Let's Read About Pets

Goldfish

PORTER COUNTY PUBLIC LIBRARY SYSTEM

Reading consultant ... consultant

WEEKLY WR READER®
EARLY LEARNING LIBRARY

Please visit our web site at: www.earlyliteracy.cc
For a free color catalog describing Weekly Reader® Early Learning Library's
list of high-quality books, call 1-877-445-5824 (USA) or 1-800-387-3178 (Canada).
Weekly Reader® Early Learning Library's fax: (414) 336-0164.

Library of Congress Cataloging-in-Publication Data

Macken, JoAnn Early, 1953-
     Goldfish / by JoAnn Early Macken.
        p. cm. — (Let's read about pets)
     Summary: A simple introduction to goldfish and how to care for them.
     Includes bibliographical references and index.
     ISBN 0-8368-3797-5 (lib. bdg.)
     ISBN 0-8368-3844-0 (softcover)
     1. Goldfish—Juvenile literature.   [1. Goldfish.   2. Pets.] I. Title.
   SF458.G6M24   2003
   639.3'7484—dc21   2003045019

First published in 2004 by
Weekly Reader® Early Learning Library
330 West Olive Street, Suite 100
Milwaukee, WI 53212 USA

Editorial: JoAnn Early Macken
Art direction: Tammy Gruenewald
Page layout: Katherine A. Goedheer

Printed in the United States of America

1 2 3 4 5 6 7 8 9 07 06 05 04 03

Note to Educators and Parents

Reading is such an exciting adventure for young children! They are beginning to integrate their oral language skills with written language. To encourage children along the path to early literacy, books must be colorful, engaging, and interesting; they should invite the young reader to explore both the print and the pictures.

Let's Read About Pets is a new series designed to help children learn about the joys and responsibilities of keeping a pet. In each book, young readers will learn interesting facts about the featured animal and how to care for it.

Each book is specially designed to support the young reader in the reading process. The familiar topics are appealing to young children and invite them to read — and re-read — again and again. The full-color photographs and enhanced text further support the student during the reading process.

In addition to serving as wonderful picture books in schools, libraries, homes, and other places where children learn to love reading, these books are specifically intended to be read within an instructional guided reading group. This small group setting allows beginning readers to work with a fluent adult model as they make meaning from the text. After children develop fluency with the text and content, the book can be read independently. Children and adults alike will find these books supportive, engaging, and fun!

— Susan Nations, M.Ed., author, literacy coach,
and consultant in literacy development

Goldfish are not all gold. They may be black, red, white, or other colors.

They may have
spots, stripes, or
other patterns.
Their bodies are
covered with
scales.

scales

Some goldfish have slim bodies and long, slender tail **fins**. These fish can be fast swimmers.

fins

Some goldfish
have thick bodies
and large,
rounded tail fins.
These fish may
not swim as fast.

Goldfish breathe with **gills**. Gills take oxygen from the water.

gills

To keep goldfish, you need an aquarium, or tank. Be sure to keep the tank clean.

Goldfish like to hide. Give your fish places to hide. Put rocks, plants, and ornaments in your tank.

Goldfish cannot
close their eyes.
When they sleep,
they sink down
in the water
and stay still.

Keep your goldfish healthy. Feed them fish food flakes. Feed them twice every day — but not too much!

Glossary

gills — organs for taking oxygen from water

ornaments — objects used to decorate

oxygen — a gas in the air that people and animals breathe

patterns — designs or forms

For More Information

Fiction Books

Kitamura, Satoshi. *Goldfish Hide-and-Seek.*
    New York: Farrar, Straus and Giroux, 1997.
Kroll, Virginia L. *Helen the Fish.* Morton Grove, Ill.:
    Albert Whitman, 1992.

Nonfiction Books

Miller, Michaela. *Goldfish.* Des Plaines, Ill.:
    Heinemann Interactive Library, 1998.
Walker, Pam. *My Goldfish.* New York:
    Children's Press, 2001.

Web Sites
Common Goldfish

www.enchantedlearning.com/subjects/fish/printouts/
Goldfishprintout.shtml
Common Goldfish facts and printout to color from
Enchanted Learning

Index

About the Author

JoAnn Early Macken is the author of two rhyming picture books, *Sing-Along Song* and *Cats on Judy*, and three other series of nonfiction books. She teaches children to write poetry, and her poems have appeared in several children's magazines. A graduate of the M.F.A. in Writing for Children and Young Adults program at Vermont College, she lives in Wisconsin with her husband and their two sons.